M000074212

CAT-ASTROPHE

CAT-ASTROPHE

WILLOW CREEK PRESS®

Published by Willow Creek Press, Inc.
P.O. Box 147, Minocqua, Wisconsin 54548

Photo Credits:
P15 © Michael Westhoff/istockphoto; P21 © Stacey Newman/istockphoto; P24 © Grigory Bibikov/istockphoto; P27 © Arseniy45/istockphoto; P29 © MarynaVoronova/istockphoto; P34 © liveostockimages/istockphoto; P36 © Michelle Gibson/istockphoto; P37 © SilviaJansen/istockphoto; P42 © sdominick/istockphoto; P49 © Sergeeva/istockphoto; P52 © anders boman/istockphoto; P54 © sae1010/istockphoto; P55 © sdominick/istockphoto; P62 © AlexSava/istockphoto; P68 © PhotoJet5/istockphoto; P69 © c-foto/istockphoto; P70 © Vampirica/istockphoto; P73 © sduben/istockphoto; P74 © kozorog/istockphoto; P77 © HIT1912/istockphoto; P83 © jtyler/istockphoto; P85 © dennisvdw/istockphoto; P87 © ADeslo/istockphoto; P90 © Emir Memedovski/istockphoto All other photos © shutterstock

Printed in China

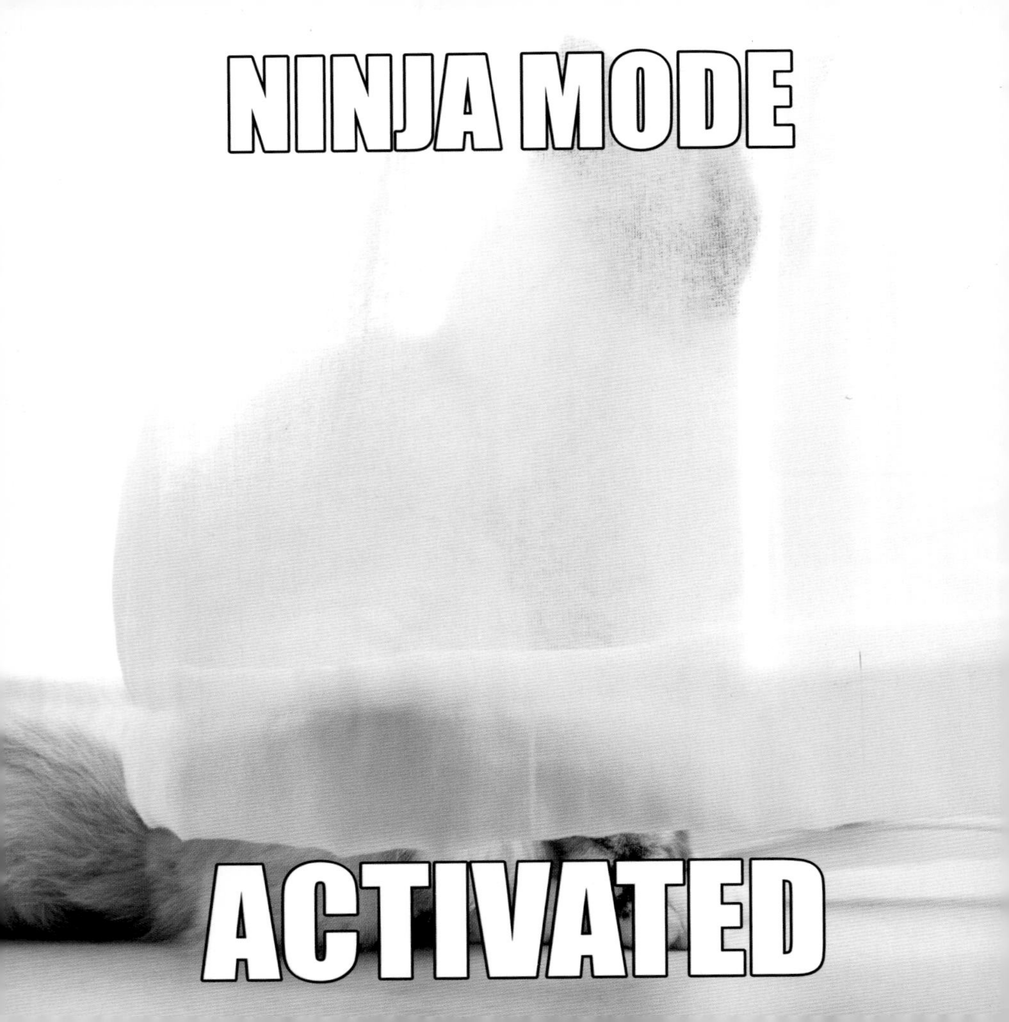
NINJA MODE
ACTIVATED

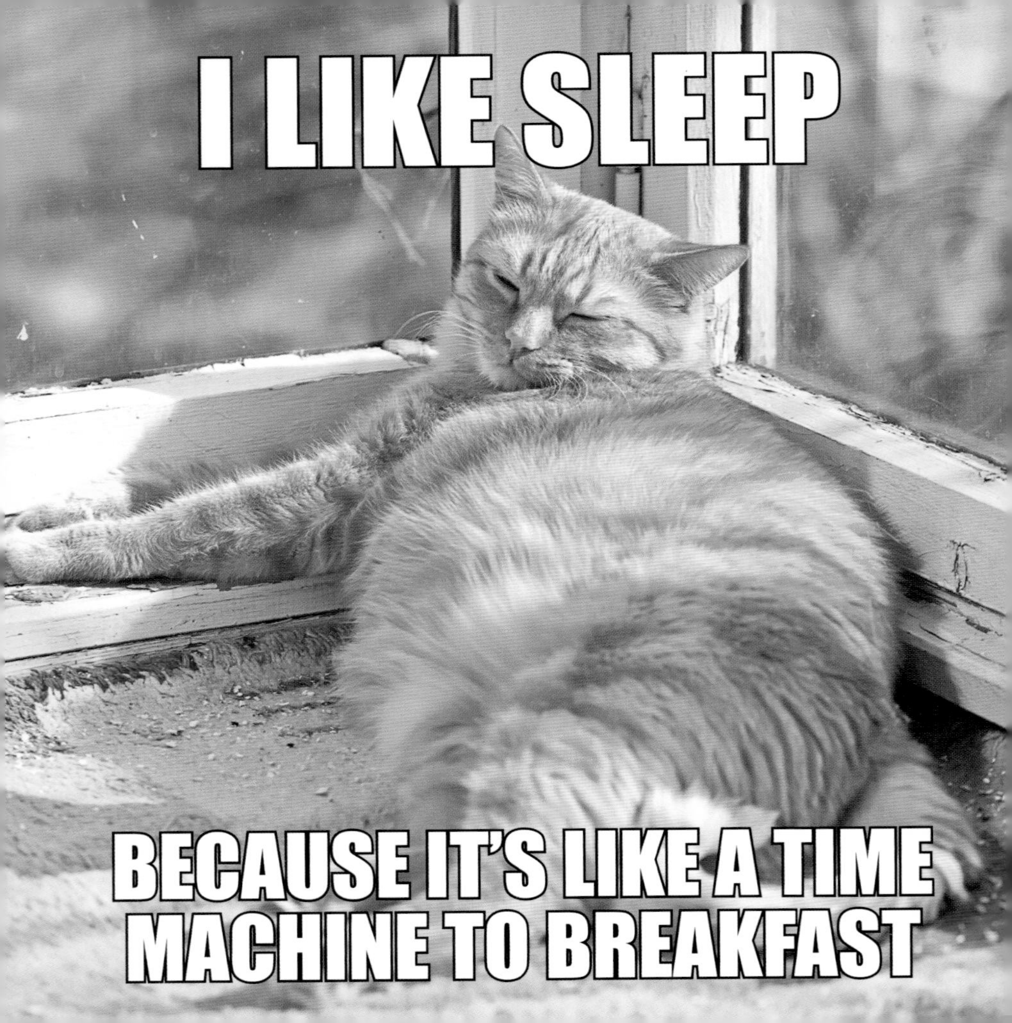
I LIKE SLEEP
BECAUSE IT'S LIKE A TIME MACHINE TO BREAKFAST

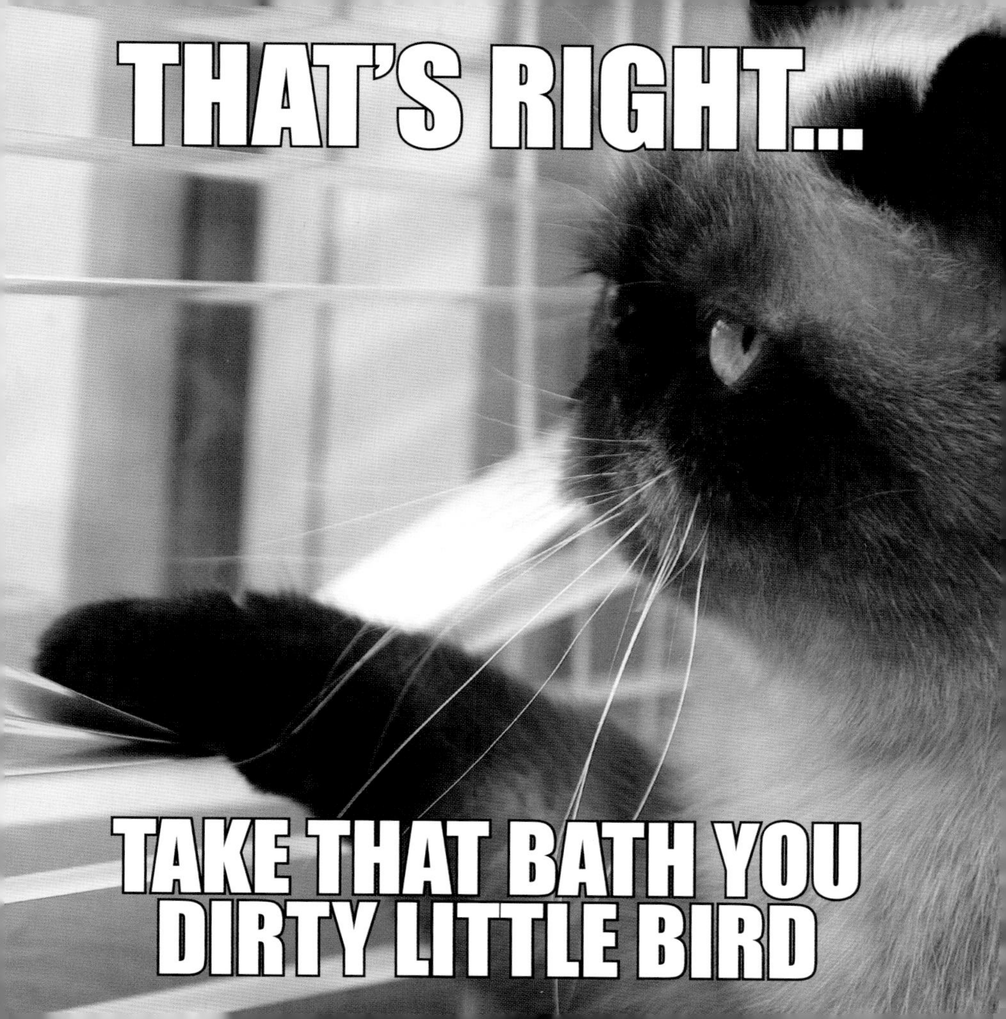
THAT'S RIGHT...
TAKE THAT BATH YOU
DIRTY LITTLE BIRD

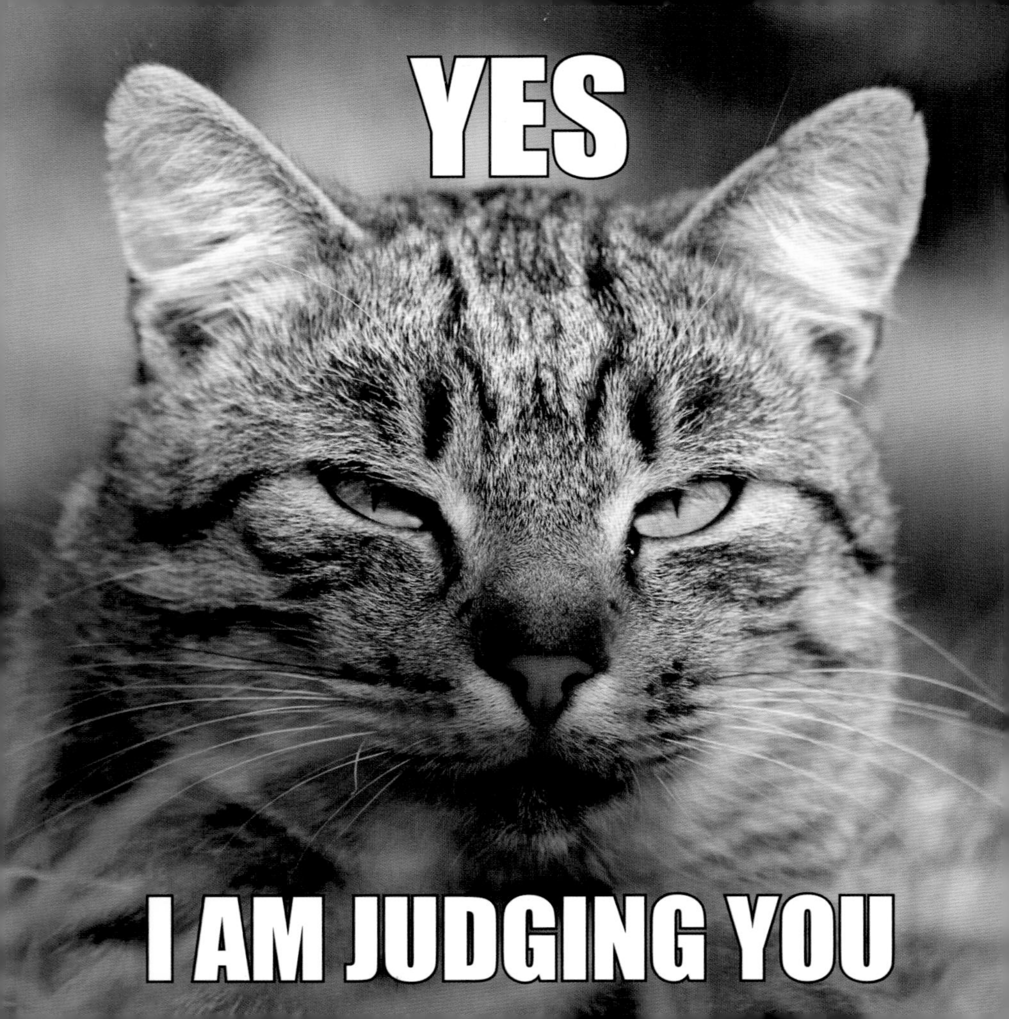
YES
I AM JUDGING YOU

I'M A CAT

I'M PURRFECT

ATE 4 BOXES OF THIN MINTS

NOT FEELING THIN AT ALL

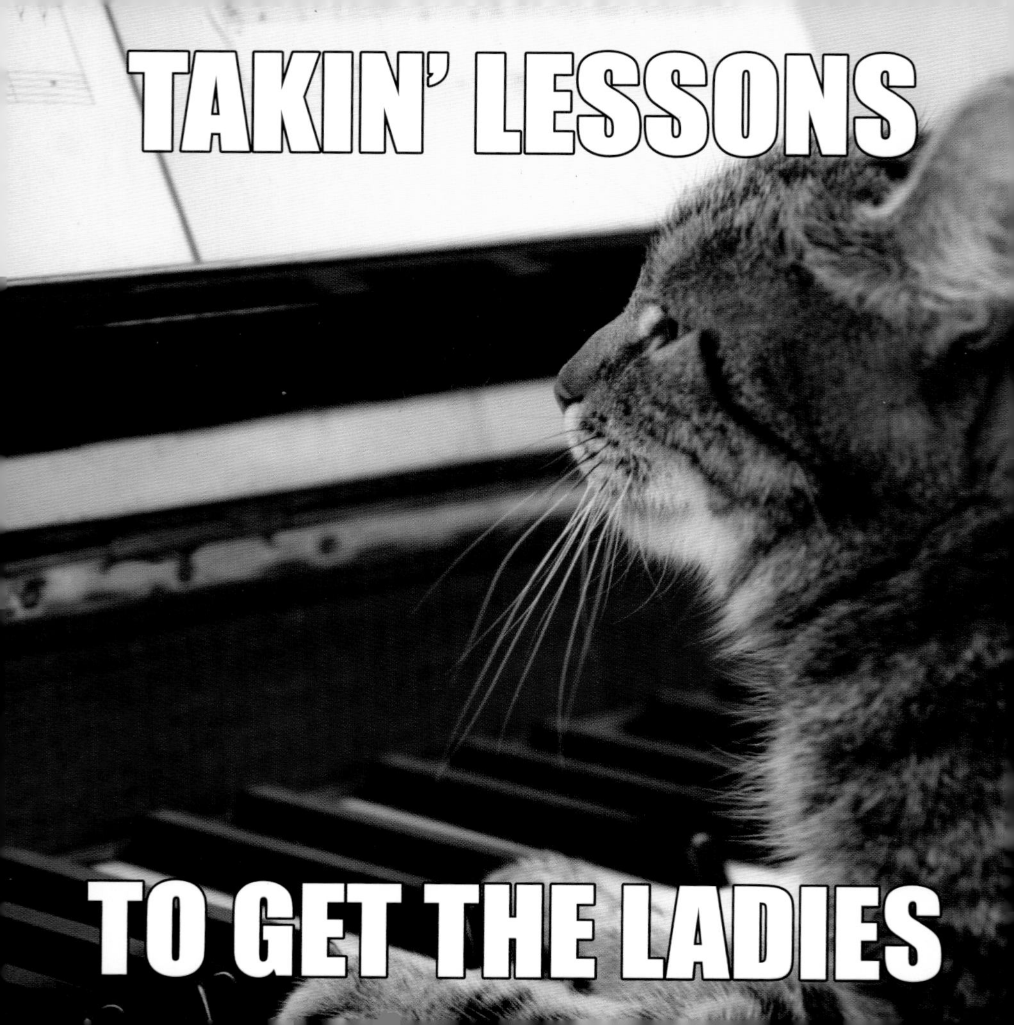
TAKIN' LESSONS
TO GET THE LADIES

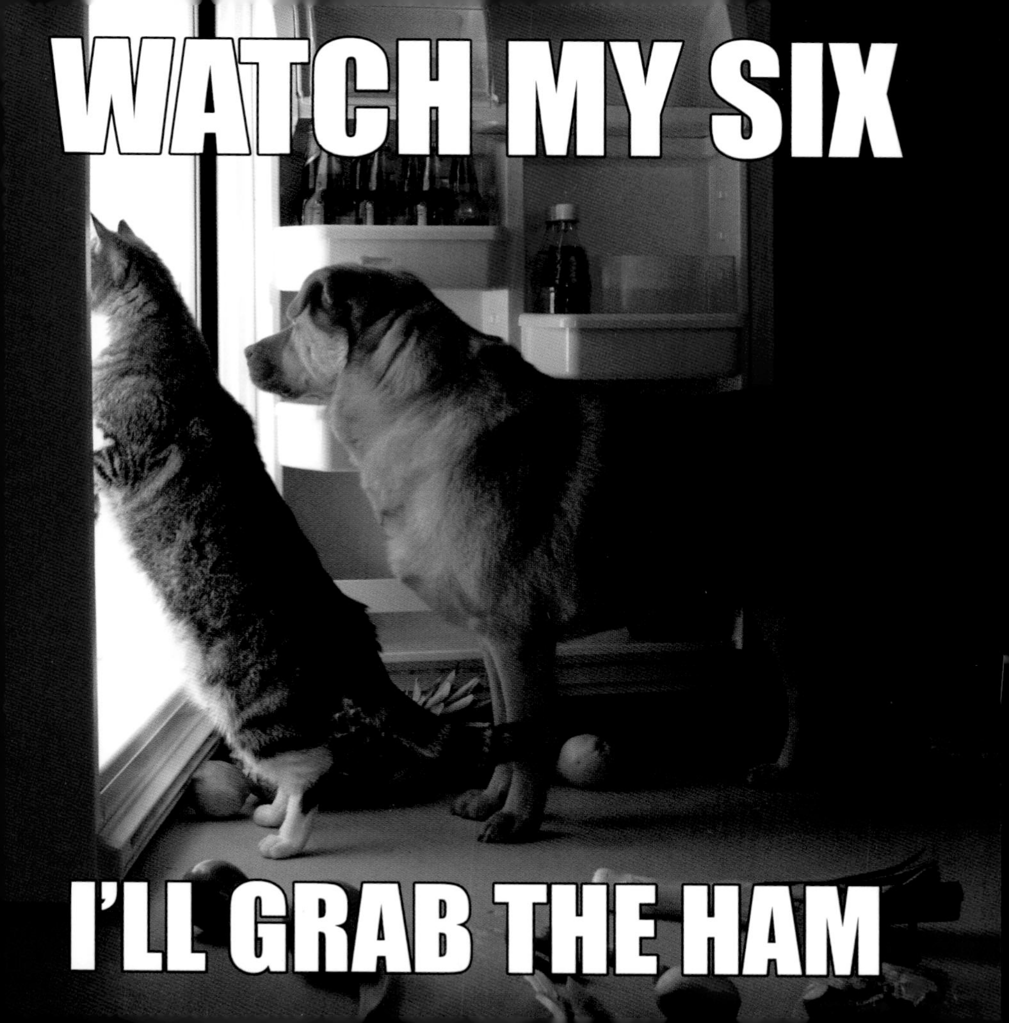
WATCH MY SIX
I'LL GRAB THE HAM

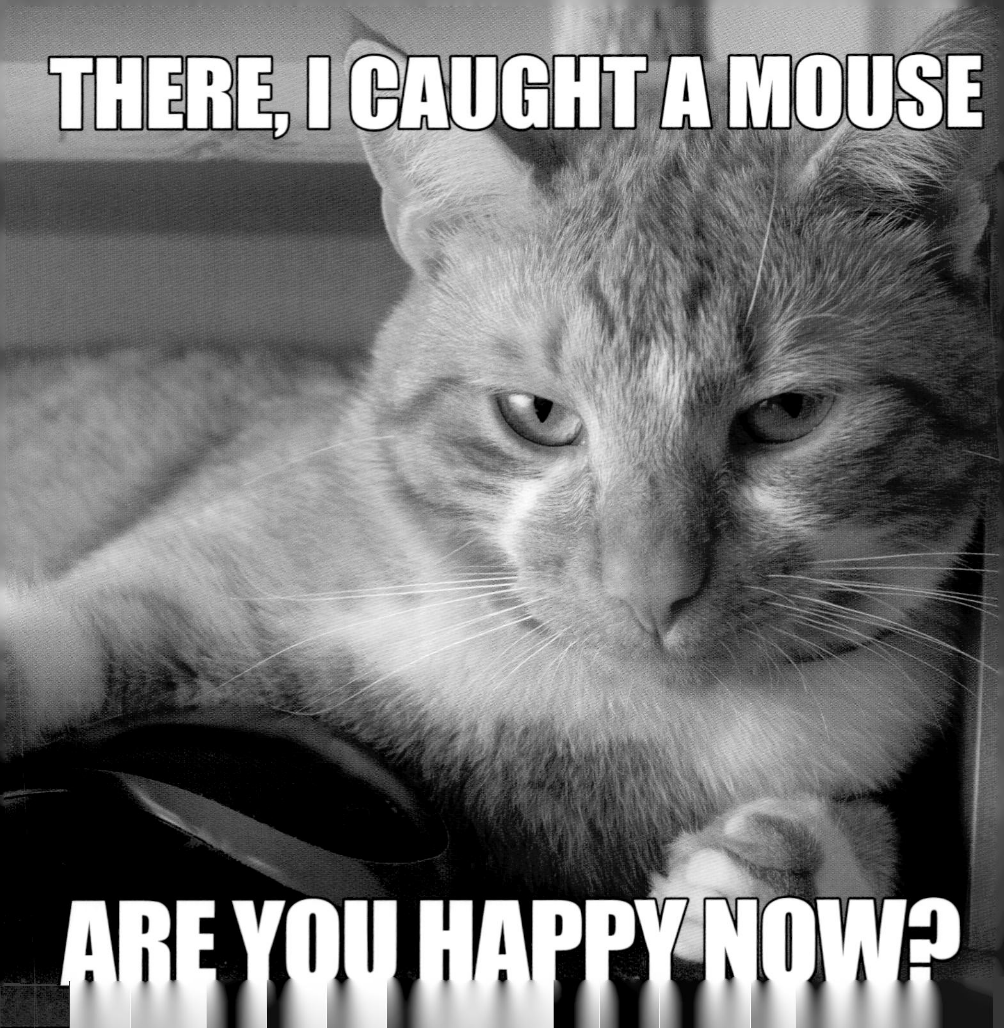
THERE, I CAUGHT A MOUSE
ARE YOU HAPPY NOW?

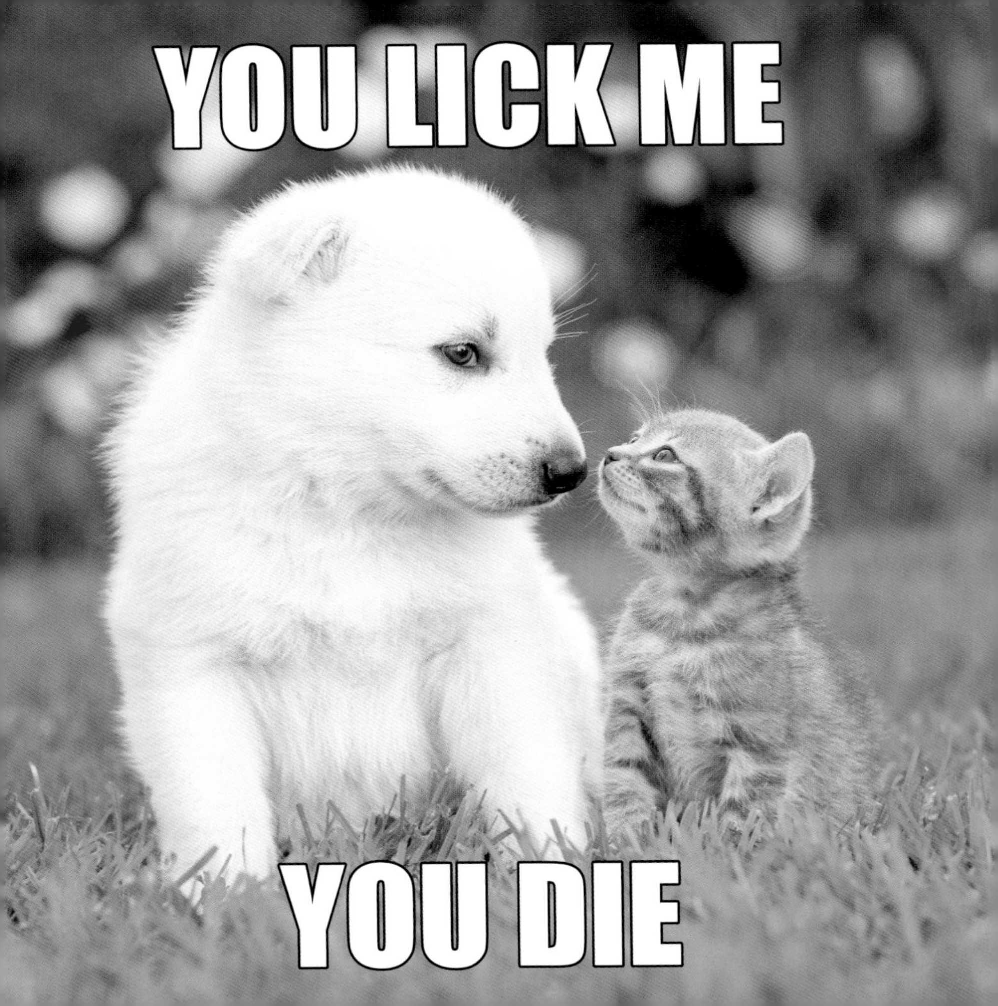
YOU LICK ME
YOU DIE

MOTIVATION

LEVEL: 0

LEAVE NO CRUMB BEHIND

TUESDAY IS

MONDAY'S UGLY SISTER

YELLOW SNOW
IS WHAT?!?

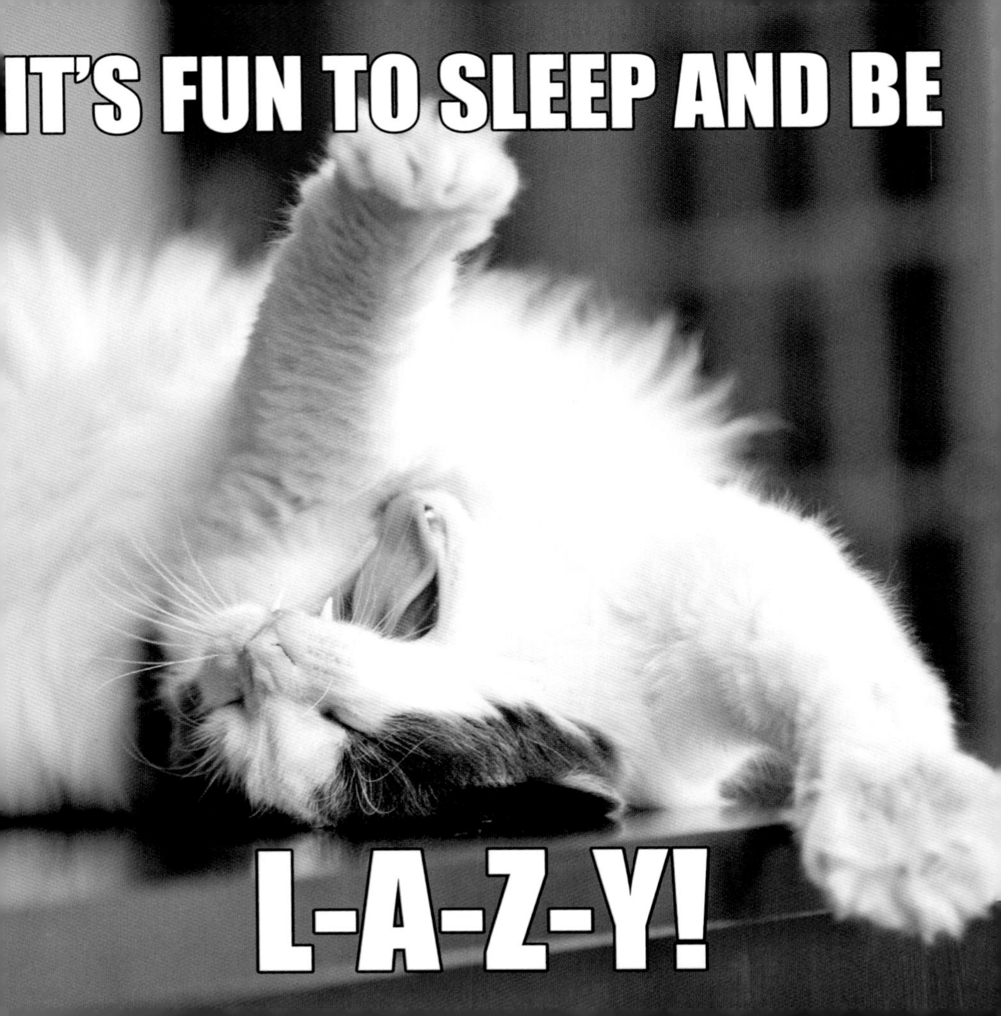
IT'S FUN TO SLEEP AND BE
L-A-Z-Y!

BEING DUMPED AFTER

PAYING FOR DINNER

GET HAIR ON CLEAN LAUNDRY

CHECK!

THE MOMENT YOU REALIZE

THEY FORGOT TO TURN ON PARENTAL CONTROLS

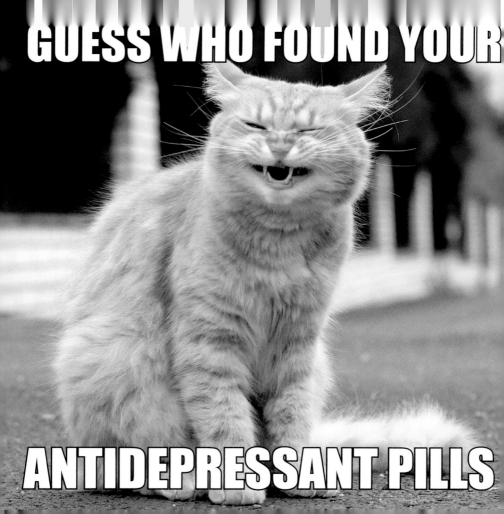

I WANT TO SLEEP ON THE KEYBOARD

BUT NO ONE IS USING THE COMPUTER

GIVE ME A HIGH PAW!

THERE WILL BE CUDDLES

THERE IS NO ESCAPE

OH I'M SORRY

WERE YOU TRYING TO PRINT SOMETHING?

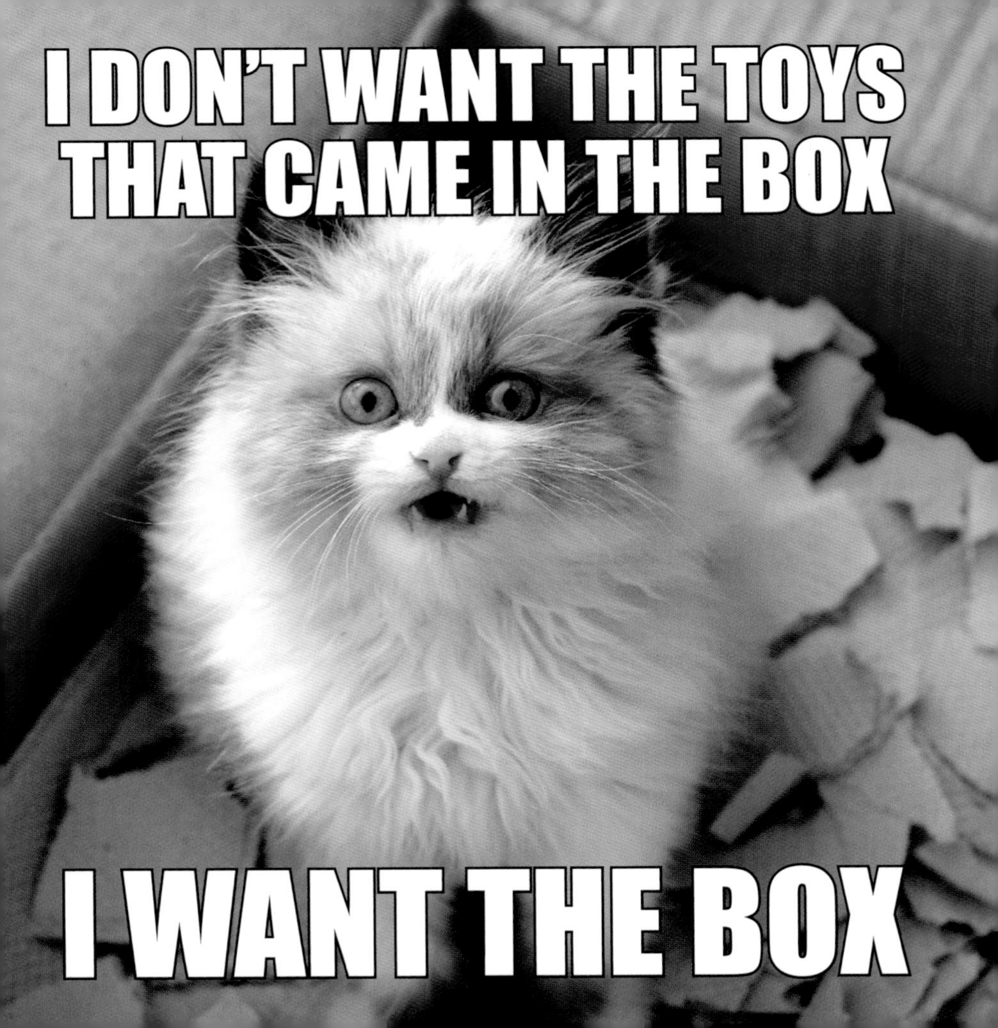
I DON'T WANT THE TOYS
THAT CAME IN THE BOX
I WANT THE BOX

DEAR GOD, PLEASE GRANT ME THE STRENGTH

TO CRUSH MY ENEMIES

TIS I, COLONEL MUSTARD

I BELIEVE IT WAS MRS. WHITE, IN THE STUDY, WITH A CANDLESTICK

MY GIFT TO YOU IS...

MYSELF

IF I JUST KEEP LOOKING CUTE

THEY'LL SURELY BLAME THE DOG

HAD A HAIRBALL

MADE IT TO THE CARPET ON TIME

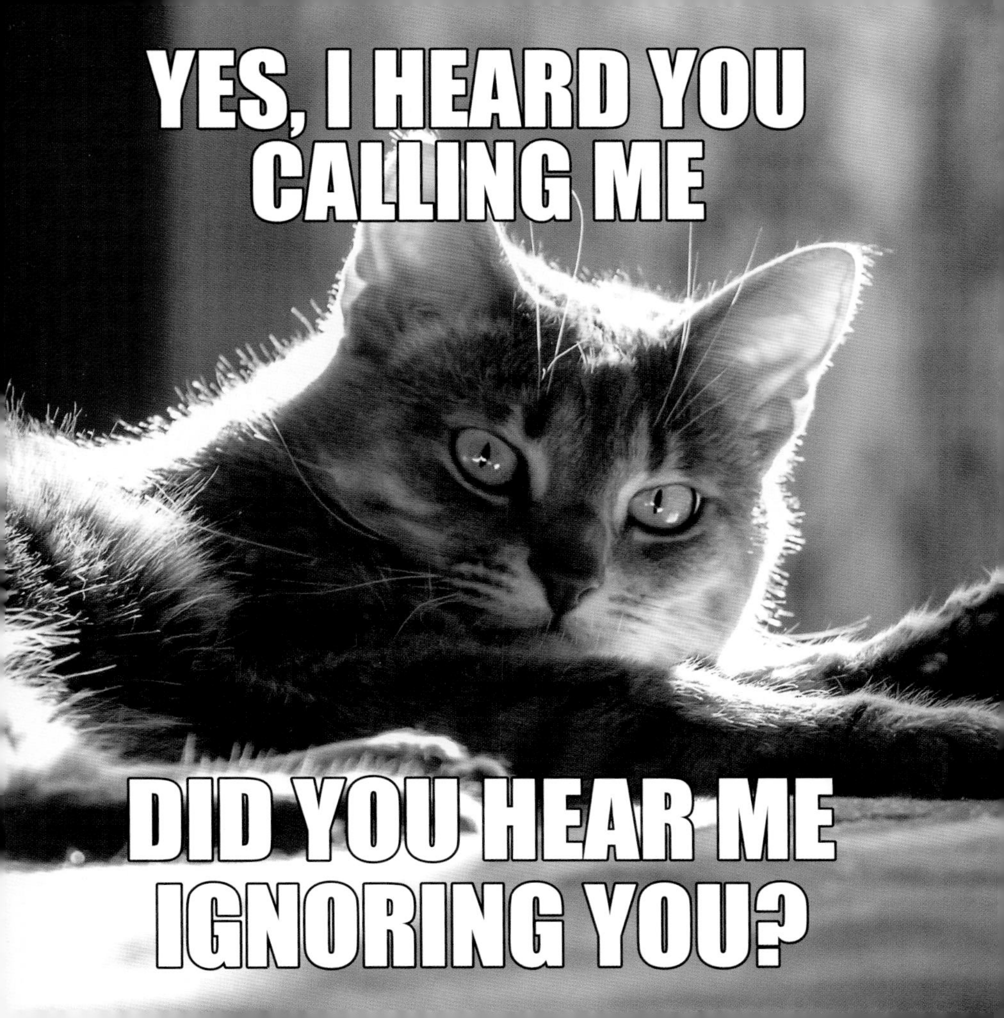
YES, I HEARD YOU CALLING ME
DID YOU HEAR ME IGNORING YOU?